BOOKS BY JOHN DAVIS JR.

Growing Moon, Growing Soil: Poems of My Native Land

The Boys of Men

Middle Class American Proverb

Hard Inheritance

The Places That Hold

poems

John Davis Jr.

THE PLACES THAT HOLD

John Davis Jr.

© 2021

POETRY

ISBN 978-1-934894-68-2

FOREWORD: Michael Presley Bobbitt

BOOK DESIGN: EK Larken

COVER PHOTO: Eye Scout Images

AUTHOR PHOTO: Heather Reuter

PUBLISHED BY

EASTOVER
— PRESS —
Rochester, Massachusetts

www.EastOverPress.com

The Places That Hold

HISTORICAL NOTE

Many poems in chapter three of this volume are based upon
witness testimony, research, and official records from the Dozier
Reform School for Boys in Marianna, Florida. The school was
permanently closed in 2014 after the bodies of 55 boys were
discovered in anonymous graves on the school grounds.
Records indicate that 41 other boys died while under the school's
care. Most of the boys imprisoned at Dozier lacked fathers or
strong father-figures in their lives.

Some chapter three poems are respectfully written in the personae
of those (both living and deceased) who endured conditions at
Dozier. Certain names have been fictionalized for privacy.
Even today, the school's survivors, many of whom were merely
truants and lesser offenders, suffer PTSD and night terrors from
events that took place during their stay at Dozier.

This book is dedicated to them.

CONTENTS

FOREWORD

When I feel myself adrift, I try to locate the corner posts and geodetic marks that remind me of what is true and real—family, faith, strong sweet tea, the carpenter's tools I inherited from my father, low-tide Cedar Key mud. Add to this list the poetry of John Davis Jr., which not only reminds me of the nurturing culture of Old Florida, but leads me into its intricacies with a steady, guiding hand.

Beginning with *Middle Class American Proverb,* flowing through *Hard Inheritance,* and now here in *The Places That Hold,* Mr. Davis' writing helps me set aside the whirl and hum of the changing digital age and instantly reminds me of what's important in my life; the four corners of where I come from are made clearer through the lens of these wonderful poems.

There is a rare authenticity in Mr. Davis' writing—so clearly the honest toil of someone whose life's work has been to catalogue, protect, and elucidate the guts of a changing place before it becomes unrecognizable. It feels weird to keep calling him Mr. Davis, even for the sake of this foreword. I can't do it any longer because I know John. I've known John since we were incoming freshmen at Florida Southern College, a fancy private school where two kids from the orange grove were out of their element and floundering together. This detail is only relevant here because it serves to further establish John's bona fides as a consummate chronicler of our culture. While I flopped from one shiny thing to the next, trying to find something to be about, John never did. Even in our tiny dorm rooms, his sense of place and identity were as steadfast as anything can be in Florida, and you will see this calm authority throughout *The Places That Hold.*

They hold because John is holding them for us.

This is all not to say that John's poetry is mere nostalgia. Such a description would hollow out the real purpose of these poems, which is not to cling to the sentiment of a bygone era, but to recognize and appreciate the foundation piers under the house, even as the siding and roof is occasionally blown away in a storm and replaced. You need not look far or invest much time to see if I'm telling you the truth. Open the first poem in this book, *Tractor Ghosts*, invest the 30 seconds it takes to read its 15 lines, and if you aren't turned inside out by the story of a grandson fumbling the operation of his grandfather's old tractor, look me up, and I will buy John's book back from you, even as I worry for your immortal soul. Because when the young man in the poem says, "Grandfather, I am driving your memory back to the shed," he's not just pontificating on lineage and legacy, he's also trying to drive the damn tractor and failing at it. The grandfather's memory is not just a dead thing to remember but a set of instructions to make the machine work. John's writing, here more than ever, is an instruction manual on how to make modern life work, not in spite of our fading old Florida traditions but because of them. The grandfather's memory is alive because of its practical application in the young man's life.

This kind of storytelling doesn't always feel good in your stomach, and it shouldn't. *The Places That Hold* braves to tackle some of the darkest memories of our shared Florida history, never gratuitously, always unflinching, and with an eye toward understanding how we are formed and influenced by them. I have read the poem in this book, *Laundry Duty, 3 Am*, maybe twenty times now, trying to shake it loose from me, trying to soften the horror of it by repetition. I'm thankful there exists the kind of storytelling in these poems that cannot be shaken loose. You will be thankful, too, to have found this book and to have discovered a masterful storyteller living here among us in the scrub pines and estuaries.

Juan Ponce de Leon never found or even looked for the fountain of youth. De Soto's historical contribution to Florida is as false as Main Street in Disney World or the fantasy that it never freezes here. Key West stopped being Key West a long time ago, and you can barely get an oyster from Apalachicola Bay anymore, but there are yet places in Florida that continue to hold, and my friend John's poetry is here to lead you through them, be they on the map or tucked away in our collective memory.

Attaboy, John. Not bad for a kid from Wauchula.

MICHAEL PRESLEY BOBBITT
CEDAR KEY, FLORIDA, 2021

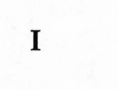

I

Tractor Ghosts

Grandfather, I am driving your memory back to the shed.
Your tractor's power steering is shot, and navigation demands
a farmer's muscle to raise specter-gray clouds of soil.

Diesel smoke stays in this baggy work shirt, and it triggers
your lessons: *solenoid, starter, alternator, filter,* and all
the anatomy I'd need to keep your machine intact.

Like a staggering November deer, this mechanical animal
is wounded—dripping red liquid down every middle,
its bleating gears draw a DNA spiral of vultures.

Everything falters. Even with tools of lineage and legacy,
I cannot pour—I cannot keep—life inside it. To get enough
jump for juice, I charge the battery overnight and pray.

Stubborn, it will crank again, sensing the wrong spirit controls
its way. These unscarred fingers, these lineless eyes know city
currency, university books. They fail the stiff-turning wheel.

My Grandfather's Exhibit

He called that barn wall full of tools
he knew he'd never use again his museum:

Rusted ice tongs, missing-tined pitchfork,
cattle brand for his cowless farm,
an awl with bits gone brown in their dusty box.

When work aged into a relic, he padlocked
it all and left the dark to do its job—
to blind those items, to make them forget his hands.

After he passed, we unfastened the hasp
and cast a rectangle of morning
over his cache of labor, his hold.

Thinned by neglect, they hung and rested still,
their heads and hinges crumbling with release.

Avenging Eve

Dusk, and my grandmother, the stronger woman,
is thrusting her small garden hoe at a green snake.
The only good one is a dead one, she says, striking.

She renders the creature into twitching tubes.
Its dilated eye is scared slitherless, growing glassier
while the yard dogs panic, wondering what's next.

Cold apple-red blood spots the south porch concrete.
She rinses the serpent's defeat away
with her green garden hose as crows

gather in the grove, awaiting pieces
of a small housewife's victory
over history, over blame, over fear.

Letter to Ancestors

I am writing you back
into existence: an ink
resurrection so permanent
even history's rising heat
cannot fade you.

Your solar spirits' motes
will not be left to circle
in the divided light
of upstairs blinds or to settle
into the carpet's plush pile.

Here you move in monochrome:
reanimated into square
capitals, squat vowels,
and thick punctuations—
pauses like windowsill wasps.

Ode to Inherited Ties

Because all fashions return, I keep them
suspended from silver hooks behind the closet door.
They sway and trail: oblong pennants of a lost contest.
Too broad and fatly patterned for the present,
one day they will be bound again when times tire
of thinner, quieter strips or empty collars
gaping like unfed mouths gasping their last.

In the final picture the church took, grandfather,
you stare straight ahead in a deacon's dark suit
anchored by striped blue cloth held fast
in a pointed double Windsor aiming
toward your servant heart—that same
ordained organ you passed on to me like so
many other kept orders in Sunday silk.

The Dying Angler's Timepiece

The drops of river caught in my father's watch
surface daily at noon, lured to the crystal
by his pulsing wrist's friction, a motion
like casting for trout, but more tremulous—
age ravages nerve lines, sending tics
where measured, certain degrees once reigned.

The drops are trapped. By night, they hover
among miniscule axles and free-floating cogs.
Clockwork glistens with ancient water taken
by accident from a dark and downstream hole—
the one he said *never failed all these years*—
its irresistible eddies circling with fish.

The drops are rusting the moving parts, though
slowly. Like so many bed-stones tumbled smooth,
every wheel and tooth will one day round off—
caressed into corrosion, their reeling will stop.
For now, the face is obscured; numbers
and hands blur beneath liquid prisms.

Elementary Football Girls, 1987
for Bonnie and Charlene

We clipped and snugged our belts of yellow flags
to struggle in autumn like our forgotten mothers:
We shoved against similar sweat
while watching over our shoulders for shadows
of crooked passes we desired to fall our way—
unleashed rocking spirals so brief above,
catching them meant a Hail-Mary miracle
stopped only by hesitance, by fear
of becoming too much like men.

At home, perspiring over stoves or in clothesline sunlight,
the women who raised us held metal between their lips:
pins, spoons, and aluminum words unspoken.
We shouted *I'm open! I'm open!* to a backfield boy
in a loose-fitting sweatshirt, only to watch his throw
wobble past our pigtails and bounce from the chest
of a Scott or a Joey or a what's-his-name from Zolfo.
Our extended hands fell like pots or baskets left
empty except for the dirty low-five of next-time promises.

Finding my Mother's Grapette Bottle

In the armadillo dark beneath our farmhouse,
I discover your six-ounce sin adorned in cursive:
Wartime only-child, you smuggled cool soda
away from grown-up glares and cavity warnings.

Not curved but tapered, this glass vessel
sweated in humid shade where you played
spy or ringleader, depending on radio
news or dramas voiced too deeply.

Here, where plated creatures dig for safety,
you swigged secrets purple as Eden's fruits
before afternoon rains and adolescence
set in, spurring growth, quenching ancient thirsts.

II

Slingshot Prophecies

The stretch and launch of untargeted pennies
planted our land in bronze. Pinching leather over
Lincoln, we pulled hard as our elastic muscles allowed.
Stray cents dinged a neighbor's tractor, a shed's tin roof.

After whirring copper blurred through cloud-ripped denim skies,
we never knew: Heads or tails? Sand wouldn't render decisions
for aimless, thriftless boys who shot for the gleam, for the humming
curve—trajectories bent by farm wind and country fate.

When mason-jar change ran out, we tried our fathers' beer caps.
Their teeth chewed the air, whistled dissonance like Saturday
cat calls followed by a Sunday church organ:
...my treasures are laid up/ somewhere beyond the blue...

A thousand rains later, the circles emerged: Green discs
of In-God-We-Trust money and razor-lipped reminders
of drunken dads. Each offered again their weathered choices
to older boys who'd once spun away from this soil.

Craft Men

Our Cub Scouts den mother forced us to fashion
cowboys from pipe cleaners, pirates from clothespins.
Tender fingers turned white wood and fuzzy wire
into characters colored by vinegar-scented markers.

Real men she called them: gunslingers, swashbucklers
rainbowed with glitter and dime-store puffy paint
until their figures twinkled and glowed in the dark
of small-town bedrooms clad in deep reds and blues.

When we pressed our figures into battle, their decorations
flecked loose, embedded in fingertip ridges
until a new Tuesday when we would repair them—
splintered, malformed in a land of bandanas and sashes.

Thriftway Ponies

You don't know who's touched those things Aunt Margie says
after *No.* She will not trust their spray-painted teeth,
their danger-red bodies and black metal saddles.

I'd seen my friends take the quarter-fed gallop
driven by lurching levers and gears
concealed beneath a blue base marked *FUN!*

She'd seen sucker-sticky fingers clutching
plastic reins. *Downtown is covered in germs.*
She scowled at short-lived laughter, mechanical groans.

On the sundries aisle, she lets me choose
her front porch light bulbs   *Yellow or white?*
and her bedroom clock batteries   *Copper or silver?*

Beyond the automatic doors and out-of-order
Cheerwine machine, I still hear the horses
running nowhere, the pointless noise of play.

Lawn Bodies

Dwight called me *dumpster bastard*
with too much truth in his voice.

So I struck him hard in the jaw
and he fell, hitting his blond head
on our front-yard rain tree's trunk.

> He didn't get up. I ran.

My stepfather, preparing to mow,
found Dwight coldcocked minutes later,
and fireman-carried him
to his grandparents next door.

> *Boys…What can you do?*

After icing the headache,
Dwight came back, invited me to the dirt
hole he'd dug behind his Pa-paw's shop.
Red plastic ninjas and dollar-store commandos

filled fingernail-crafted caves in its walls.
Soon, they would drown in a garden-hose flood,
lose ground to die-cast cars and trucks
until we filled the void with leveled soil.

> Another year, and we wouldn't cross the fence.

The rain tree sheds its yellow blooms,
and they are breeze-rolled over our older lawns
before settling, dispersed or crushed on the road.

Biohazard Summer

We endangered ourselves
because no one else would
in the soft-hedged suburbs
where clotheslines were banned.

Truth-or-daring by the lake
where hospital waste
was dumped, we choked
on smoke from contraband:

Lifted cigarettes and illegal
fireworks we'd found by luck
in all the wrong places.
Not unlike our hands

that didn't know where to go,
they fumbled and fell
in splayed and spent messes
wherever they'd land—

used up in the worst
locations where red bags
and bed pans protruded
like freshly hung sheets in wind.

A Father's Good Night

My pats on your back
are knocks on the door
to a smoother future
I know you will be.

You will sleep only to my tilt
and sway, my invented
lullaby like gate hinges in wind
closing a heavy day's hard passage.

You seek five o'clock shadow
assurance: the friction and height
of blown treetops—nature's notes
more baritone than Brahms.

In the crib, you sigh from lungs
that protested your mother's
kneading fingers, softer
shoulder, perfect pitch.

Daddy's child, your closed eyes
form smiling crescents as pleasant
storms of dreams descend
and roll in the darkness.

Creek Wading with a Young Son

Arriving by bike, we know to whisper like the woods:
This stream's soft trill and the wind's slow travel
through pines drown the drone of highway lanes
beyond the palmetto-frond hands opening toward water.

Predator, provider: This anonymous tributary
takes and gives alike as our four bare feet
bring clouds from its white sand bottom—swirling rising
residue stirs south, settles back beneath water.

Your passage here disproves ancient philosophy:
I am the nameless man who stepped in the same time
twice thanks to your smaller, faster-filling tracks.
My deeper plunges do not slow this aging water.

In sunlit pockets along the dark-patched course,
shadow fish dart like memories—there, gone.
But we have neither hooks nor bread today,
so black scales brush our foreign ankles underwater.

Your sunken toes discover some animal's rib
and like a tribesman, you lift it, fling it forward.
It skips, ripples holes in two distant points
before rocking and sinking in new familiar water.

The Talk: Youngest Son

By the backyard pond where you liked to fold
my calendar pages into sharp-beaked planes,
we sit a hand-width apart on a pollen-green bench
to speak of procreation and its parts. No more storks.

Not even a metaphor of birds. You deserve
truth laid plain. You, who yesterday
floated a milk-carton ship to the far shore, hear
how humans are made: Biology.

Your eyes widen after knowledge, reflect
like those of the nearby heron guarding its nest.
Our pond ripples purple with evening
as current crosses a once-still body.

For a Cautious Son, 13

Some limbic instinct
within you recalls birth:
the slick beige cord wrapped twice
around your neck, strangling
you blue before the uncoiling,
the toothless inhale, the scream.

You will not Tarzan
across the creek like your
younger brother who swings
wildly on vines, awaiting
the fibrous rip, the immersion.

Hollering broken vowels, he whirls
over rippled red-brown water again,
dropping halfway for a splash
before surfacing, gasping laughter.

I will not tell you today
I was handed the silver shears
in the delivery room.

Too soon, I will cut
you free to the world again.

Oh, how I wish you'd jump.

Violin Boy

I drop euros in your case daily:
the ones I won't give to the footless beggar
who colors his fresh sterile gauze with red marker.
You are tall and young enough to remind me
of my own son, and your song is more fiddle
than concerto. It summons some home
in this Lisbon I visit. You nod and smile,
play toward my wife—your chin never leaving
its black rest while your brown eyes say *Obrigado*.
The ankle-nubbed man shakes his cup: No music.

An Older Son's Fear

To reach the clearest creek, we risk the snakes
among palmettos. You fear rattle, hiss,
and slither, Momma's boy—tall as I—stepping
without crushing. Your gait is that of minefields.
Cautious, you will not stripe your legs in red
from saw-toothed stems, but your silent tread,
no crackle, no pressure, will let the reptiles sleep.

Bare-shinned, you stir one fattening in afternoon, meet
its hooded eyes, jump from a forked tongue's flicker
before running, forgetting forest floor dangers
with every pound of sole and heart. You explode
these woods with careless clamor. Your ankles bleed,
torn by serrated stalks. At thickets' edge, freed
from the canopy, you breathe in the sky,

where clouds begin a twisting shift—
darkening, growing fangs.

Advice to My Son before College
Matthew 7:9-10

Question the wisdom of this world I've given you.
Inquiry curls in your inherited irises,
the finite black dots of your pupils.
Student, son, I've taught you snakes and rocks,
curves and stones I know best. But you
must seek cooler, darker, and deeper layers
of understanding. Begin with a point
bent into quandary, and finish
with certainty hard as scale, well-rounded.
Ask for more bread to catch fatter fish. Eat better.

III

Dust Workers

My sister and I built ruins
the April our father left. His bricks
became a game governed by her rules:
We have to crush them and collect the dust.
The boss says he'll be back to inspect.

With a rusty claw hammer,
we crumbled bricks into chunks,
chunks into sediment that gathered
under our fingernails and among
the backyard sycamore's roots.

Rusty haze rose into our nostrils,
infected our throats and laughter.
We heard its grit between our teeth at night.
Our knuckles swelled, and our sweat ran
lightning-jagged, fell into starbursts.

The boss never returned to check
our work, to watch us spit and decide
whose was redder. He'd never know
the creak of our toy truck loaded with powder
we dumped by the empty garage.

Abandonment Lessons

The roof's pitch will return thrown balls,
but prepare for the unpredictable
stagger, the occasional catch
in the gutter.

Wind will push your bike downhill until
you learn balance: how to center, lean
into gravity's air, never
too right, too left.

Shoelaces and neckties will fall into slop-knots:
uneven ends twisted and pinched,
tangled and forced into staying
a little while longer.

Pencils will guide your cursive into loops
that capture whitespace, points
directing the reader's eye
to crooked lines' ends.

Razor blades planted too deep will teach
proper pressure and easy stroke: curves
and patterns all yours to follow,
avoiding blood.

Whittling Lessons from an Absentee Father

Always away; never toward.

Gripping knife and stick, he teaches
how to cut with intentional leisure:
Shun the bark and push the pulp
out into the world. Avoid
a sliced thumb, a punctured gut.

Better to release the difficult
crooked twigs and knotty stems
than to pay with flesh and blood
for wood that wouldn't yield
to your carve or peel or score.

With sap and scent, pine satisfies
and shucking oaks' thick skin exposes
nature's pores and dimples beneath
the weakened hide of time:
perfect for stripping, forgetting.

My Father's Funeral Tent

Here at last is the shelter
you never taught me to pitch—
surrounded by fire-ring stones and ghost stories
foreign as the red clay they lower you under.

You will dwell in the house of this ground
long after the canvas and metal are gone,
long after this earth's camp is struck.

And I will be left to show my son
how to face north in darkness by finding
Polaris just off the Big Dipper:
a shovel of black sky, spiraling.

Statue Boys

for Todd and Michael, convicted of trespassing

We knew our names were already deader
than confederate generals erected
in gray cement at Dunson Park.

But nobody would care about curs
like us that summer of seedless
melons and faulty bike chains.

So we posed atop the platformed
columns in front of the Old Marsh Place,
raising sleeveless arms to point
long invisible sabers at some
butternut horizon we'd never see.

Protruding our pretend-medaled chests,
we awaited some darker enemy—economy,
phosphate mine labor or its blue-collar cancers—
to end seasons, break cycles,
fell us from small-town pedestals.

Typewriter Thief

Silver keys drew me in—neatly lettered and numbered circles
the size of my fingers. If only I could hear those hammers,
smell ink pressed free. Taken by its store display, I sought
a rhythm of permanence: the striking discharge of my name.

Once cops found the Remington in my neighbor's shed, they said
That boy, as if nobody else would want black applause
from a curious carriage's well-oiled melody
played on paper and ended with a single bell—done.

Police returned it to Mister Howard, who let it sit
because his name was already on too many buildings.
They booked me in, had me hold a sign with Courier numbers—
white holes of zeroes captured by print's hard impact.

Laundry Duty, 3 p.m.
for the boy in the dryer at Dozier Reform School

Behind his twisting white palms on the circle
of glass, we saw his wide and long-lashed
eyes trying to escape, his tumbling
red face. Bent backward,
his legs turned less-than symbols.

Ordered to ignore him, we folded white
towels end over end into tightened
squares, stacks of bleached terry cloth
thinned and threadbare from friction.

The rule-makers demanded them flat.
We forged ourselves into human irons,
exacting comfortless geometry, pressing
hard to forget burning-hair odor,
the big machine's guillotine rhythms.

The Disciplinarian

excerpted from the 2009 deposition of
Dozier School Facilitator Troy Tidwell

Smoking was a spanking offense.
So was reckless eyeballing.
When a boy talks about running
away, you've got to talk to him.

If you're not satisfied with his
answer, there's a possibility
he could get a spanking.

You tell him, *You're going down.*
He'll know where he's going without
asking. Saturday mornings,
the Colored side got it.

But I never did those.
I made my own decision
when I was asked or told to spank.

You know, if you were spanking
your own child—six or eight
licks—you use your judgment
when you're doing something like that.

Crooked Bones

Dozier Reform School, 1967

The guards will start with your fingers:
Backtalk or hesitance brings the club
shattering into your digits—un-wisecracking
you so you'll cry in front of the others.

They laughed the day they broke my humerus
and splinted it with wire coat hangers wrapped
in black tape so my skin couldn't breathe,
so I'd understand honest pain.

When a mother or two inquired about our gnarled
fingers, our curled limbs, they had a preacher
explain how the evil inside us twisted and warped,
since Satan lived in all our skeletons.

The breakings relieved you from weed clearing, though,
and you toothbrush-scrubbed bathroom tile instead—
forcing bleached bristles into straight grout lines—
a white symmetry, perfect for a while.

Climbing Cemetery Trees

for Frank, Scott, and Jimmy,
charged with "disturbing the peace"

We clambered up trunks to lifted limbs:
Green among gray names and dates.
Our forebears were buried feet away,
but we thrust upward on rungs
unimagined by those beneath.

Atop swaying magnolias, we could see
autumn-colored roofs and square holes:
our town's blackening brick chimneys.
The feed store sign: red and white check
finish line flag stuck above double doors.

That squat, ground-level place awaited
with all its business and rusting words.
Today there was shade among feather-shaped leaves
and a view of higher and clearer skies
for children perched like angels or crows.

To the 55 Uncovered

The media have forgotten you buried boys.
In light of gunfire, live matter, and cartoon craze,
they left your headlines years ago to favor
exhumed trends from 8-bit childhoods
and the snap-crack of protest posters,
the hollow fall of slogans and blame.

Have your families claimed you yet?
Do they know your bones, your stories?
Taggers, shoplifters, fighters: Shovels
disturb your rest as old guards once said
you disturbed ours. Where is justice? Academics claim
they know you now, they understand.

A silver spade cradles a gray mandible
as though it might fit a poor Yorick skull
somewhere beneath these exposed striations
of history and blackness. Buttoned down men
with brushes and magnifiers prepare to labor
in obscurity, in silence, in history.

To the 41 Dead and Undiscovered

for the unaccounted-for victims of Dozier School

They say you may be in the back forty swamp,
your bones mired in with cretaceous gators
or dissolved in the roots of cattails, lilies.
Suited and uniformed men deny you—there are
no crosses, no stone statues of limitation.

But what of your names in the records? Sable scratches
by words like *pneumonia, tuberculosis*—germs
rampant as rumors whispered about soft soil
behind a circular stand of cypresses:
A cathedral of knees marks *rest here.*

IV

Red the Cartographer
resident of Room 109, Resthaven, 1989

In sand beneath the slow swing, he draws
with his wooden cane: *Our barn was here,*
and the fields beyond were all strawberries
in winter—the ripest and fattest around.

He turns acres to inches, crops into trenches.
His stick taps holes for family dogs, swishes
and scratches for remembered pigs and chickens
penned near the tractor's shaky square.

And this circle—too big and too oval—
is home. Two stories tall, wide porch, flowerbeds.
They'll return him there one day, he swears
as March wind erases it all.

Sylvia
resident of Room 107, Resthaven, 1986

She loves the white spaces among glittering green
panels, Vanna's blue dress, and the mystery pie
slice among clickety numbers, loud chances.

Yesterday's breakfast is long forgotten, but
she talks back to Sajak when he gets too chatty:
Just call the letters! Do your job, Pat!

She equally scolds the greedy prolonger
who knows the answer but keeps on spinning;
she giggles when black bankrupt catches them.

Her family won't visit unless it's Christmas,
when they bring her a fruitcake they know
she won't eat—its colorful crumbs too much.

So she turns back to *Wheel*, tuning out before *Jeopardy!*
since all her questions are already answers.
She claps for a long, shiny car, an exotic vacation.

Preacher Earl
resident of Room 103, Resthaven, 1990

His dentures slip under lips gone thin
from apologetics. He cannot read, even
with large print lensed and highlighted,
but his memory keeps the text vibrant.

Before his teeth went, ministerial
syllables shook sinners like pounds
of the wooden-box pulpit: palms
for attention, fists for emphasis.

Sundays he tries to tell the others
about blind Bartimaeus, long-dead Lazarus,
but the sibilants fail him, and words
of The Word dribble out, leave no stain.

After Reading the Bible and Wendell Berry

Every season a deliverance:
the sky sending down its tools
to dig, to till, to plant, to reap
with work's careful pressure—creation.

Lean not on your own hoe handle.
In all your stirrings, a firm hand
harder and gentler than yours
creases this plain with redemption.

Let the rain be your rhythmic rake
today, farmer. Let it scratch out
lines and contours of care—
a topography of salvation.

Its tines fall and pull leaved earth
into landscape: striations
of nurture imprinted
by the sweep of liquid fingers.

The Old Gardener's Lament

Hang the hoe and rake. Shelve the gloves.
Fill the wheelbarrow with spades of rankest air
and push the load toward decay behind the greenhouse—
an emptied shell of hollow pots and compost.
Alert the papers: Horticulture is dead.
Suffering came in nettles and vines.
Snails sought cooler, wetter stones, hauling homes
south at a desperate desert crawl.
Snakes left trellises and stakes overtaken
by tightly wound Virginia creeper.

The lawn returns to beggar's lice;
rose beds surrender to sandspurs.
Neither sun nor clouds send their condolences.
Summer's torturing scorch remains—
brown and brittle—as stillness settles where
fanfare blooms once unfurled from soil.
Land hardens into memory, opening
stem-shaped cracks and tears in desolate dirt.
The moon wanes black, no growth left to light.
In lieu of flowers, send industry, send youth.

Uncivil Dentistry

to those who return here

Your hometown's pristine baby teeth have fallen out,
and in their holes, urban monoliths have taken root.
You forgot the whistle of the baseball field spigot
until you found some office in its red clay spot.

You expect happy whines of hinges and chains
at the park, but they've yanked all signs of swings,
recycling their metal into HVAC units and vertical blinds
filling the silver grill of a high-rise business building.

Here there are echoes, but no more basketball bounces:
Courts are crowned by a parking garage—two hundred spaces
forbidding bicycles, skateboards, or wheeled devices
of youth who yell into stairwells' throats to hear their voices.

When will all this rot? The decay of cavities
is mistaken for the dark digs of industry
as money-green smiles degrade into agonies
heard in the drone of drills, the scraping twist of pliers.

Disowning the Country
for one who will not return here

He rejects the universal rural truths
like rusted nails in a cloudy canning jar:
Relics bent by someone else's force.

Behind an expatriate grin, he hides our dialect
like warped boards we conceal back of the barn:
Too good to burn, too turned for building.

Those homesick tears held in reserves
thicken like wood glue, stick in his sockets:
Hardened to hold a gaze toward the future.

He muscles memories into rebellious reasons
like a crooked drawer that still closes flush:
Stubborn friction preserves continuing conflict.

Inland: A Breakup Letter

Map-dot of scorn and insufferable summers,
your corrals and dead ends drove me coastal.

I sought some unhemmed fringe where ragged waves
shush like a comforting bedtime mother.

Locked in by toll roads and bloodlines, your people
detest the salt and light of a shifting beach.

Your trembling livestock turn circles, confined
by barbed wire and their thinning shadows.

Brown as a horseshoe crab, the sod under hooves
feeds the frenzied stampede to nowhere.

Single-story buildings wall in Main Street
with green brass names, diminishing bricks.

Daily I press fading footprints in sand populated
by overnight shells polished and pushed ashore.

Vacation Crush, 1992

In young summer, everything spirals:
your beach house staircase, those shells
we find by drilling sand with tanned toes,
porpoises' paired rolling through deep green,
loopy smoke of dusk-lit bottle rockets.

Your face is framed by the spin of sunlight blond
as your smile becomes a curling ribbon path
toward dizzying kisses and Twistee Treat ice cream.
Even *fling* is a form of turning—
a stretched piece of circle in history's scroll.

Ironing My Wife's Scrubs

Steam breathes
through cotton pockets;
hot metal smell rises
with my prayers.

Understanding blood
may stain them, I starch
the blue sleeves anyway,
create scalpel-edge creases.

Her elderly patients will smile,
recalling bygone love pressed
with firm hope into yesteryear's
beige or olive or white.

When she returns to me, her body
has shaped the clothes: her turn,
her stretch, her strenuous elegance
perfect what once was uniform.

Before We Moved

You unfastened
our beige drapes of words,
said you wanted them to hang
in the new place
same as before
but shading different rooms
from unfamiliar views
and light that fell
in directions
we had never faced.

What did they say
again? Names of teas
and coffees in foreign tongues,
I think,
though I never cared
enough to notice
until you stripped them,
bundled them
over your arms
like you needed their warmth.

Our bared windows
spilled overcast day
through salted white panes,
across marble sills.
You sighed, tore tape,
and guessed they wanted
some better farewell
than a hard undressing
before you sealed that last
box marked *curtains*.

V

Rabbit Hunt

The Eastern Cottontail
will not run from your steps
but the pause in your stride.

That sudden silence fills
brown ears and black eyes
before his blur launches
from noon shadow, leaves
tracks: surprised faces.

Poem, I halt for you,
hoping your fright reveals
a heartbeat's fleeting line.

Found Feathers

Begin the collection
with a backyard blue jay's
fallen plume, or the beige
quill from a mockingbird.

From there, take to the woods,
and seek striped specimens lost
by hawks, or brown and black
chevrons shed by turkeys.

Avoid the frill and fluff
of fakes: craft store ostrich
or peacock phonies molded
and glued on a factory line.

Wade the creek instead,
and locate a left-behind
owl feather dropped in nocturnal
hunting where water runs life.

Let the discovered speak wisdom:
textures and colors united
but scattered like so much ambition
melted from Icarus.

Early Bird Prayers

When I, as a child, was asked to pray at breakfast,
I began with thanks for birds—the closest things
to heaven in my mind. Skies of that time
were flush with cardinals, blue jays, swallows,
and my sister whistled quail into our yard.
Powerline doves mourned evenings' pink,
and mockingbirds outsang roosters at dawn.

Nature's better angels—sound on wings—
gave rise to my first earnest words of beauty.
Over coffee today, I pray for their return,
asking once more for feathers and song:
Replace these empty skies with beaks and eyes;
send note-filled breasts to wreath-shaped nests,
press color and music again against these clouds.

Christmas Eve Bass

The freckled boy pulls warm fish from our cold pond,
feels life surging through green-striped bodies
as red gills flash in a tree-light sequence.

In Florida, lunkers strike year-round, fighting gold
hooks and glittering lures that dangle and twist
among dark recesses in underwater branches.

Like fat decorations, the largemouths hang
in wait for a shimmer, a hypnotic glow
that signals a difference, a promise.

Soon a star will appear in the east, and the boy
will release one last living ornament. He watches
it cross through darkness, dreams of its return.

Absence Lights

Papa, those three bottles you left collect
white sunbeams in our kitchen windowsill:

Within the square blue one, morning reflects
like Boca Grande summer surf—the crashing kind
that stole your gold class ring, a sunken treasure.

The globe-necked green one transforms fall afternoons
into mountain memories: Algae-slicked trails
and gray rocks patterned by lichens' ragged coats.

Winter evenings, the red one brings Christmas
early—the hue of our brick hearth overfilled
with long vacant stockings seeking plenty.

The bottles still sparkle too brightly, too empty
even for breeze to cross into *oh* and *oh* and *oh*.

The Farm Poet's Lament

Here, a thousand spirits no longer know you.
Your hands are those of a sleek urban stranger.
What good are words to this land? They fertilize
nothing, water even less. They are shabby
tributes to love of the few and the gone.
They cannot kill weeds; they cannot resurrect
sun-paled azaleas or hard crippled crops:
Oranges like knotted fists shake in hot wind.
Will these words increase the sugars in our fruit?
How will harvest measure their value and price?
What gain will come to the coffin-like mailbox?

Language must make more meaning than memory.
No verses ever fueled a red tractor.
No meter, except for the rain gauge, matters.
Legends and legacies implore: *Do something*,
so you fritter away these withering hours
with weak-legged theories and sounds of spoken breath
until the greatest inconsequence arrives.
Oh, laureate—what produce have you produced?
Where is the trailer loaded with goods you've done?
Semi-trucks pass on the road outside, but none
of them carries your relevance, minor scribe.

You cannot don the elder's hat or garments
thinned by real work's friction—too much and too rough.
Keep scribbling, you lost and shiftless creator.
Know shade, know comfort, know luxury purchased
by ancestors' passages over and through
these long middles in noonday labor so you,
oh petty and pitiful poet, could then
document their sinews and sweat with your sloth.
Be not arrogant, you dark academic,
for your learning is pathetic amid this
demanding farmland droughted by your letters.

Hear it? It mourns for one whose hands know till
and welcome the blister and ache of making.
Your precious literature is not commerce,
it is not fortune. Its syllables won't raise
leaves or limbs in silent green hallelujahs.
So why shed these markings like old corn snake skin?
They await small breezes of traveling feet
to blow away their brittle-crisp scales,
return their empty expense to failed soil,
adding some foreign and needless element
that arrives too little, too late anyway.

Rain is coming. Even it works. Falling fills
the grove with renewal while you imitate
its rhythm into words. But everyone knows
its sound—you search for the new in the common!
Lay down your pen, oh fiddler, and go secure
the barn. Make ready the fissure-filled homestead
for the good pounding you could never provide.
A house spider spins its silk in the corner,
dry as your head and paper in this shelter.
Thunder unrolls like cursive through heavy clouds,
and you straighten lightning into proper print.

Dying trees rattle and wag damp finger bones
in brittle points of blame and shame, accusing
as you scratch and plot your finite wonderings.
The rain still falls. The land goes on without you.
Every serif bares a tiny sharp tooth
severing heritage.

The Farm I've Willed You

Return when my strong ghost is gone:
When the ax-yard stump's black center
grows moss, when the barn rafters
lose my fingerprints, after every post
forgets the warmth of my work-breath.

No need to forever ask: Is this
how he did it? You know and will grow
your own ways—a touch ingrained
for your children to find and recall
the knots of your knuckles, planks of your palms.

The Poem You Need

It has broad, old trees with bear-paw leaves
offered by hands of wind onto a blue pond,
and the poet has told you these leaves are ships
of a season, smaller Argos floating toward winter.

Winter will mean death as it does in a poem,
and you'll ponder mortality—your life as leaf-boat
crossing this finite and funny-shaped body, driven
by holy breath wholly beyond your rudder stem.

Your sadness will be rich and brief
like boyhood butterscotch in church,
and your eyes will leave the page as you sigh,
content with humanity still sweet on your tongue.

Later you'll attempt your own poem and some
of those same words will slip into your stanzas,
unmoored from branches in the brain, placed
upon a rippled plain to begin another voyage.

Acknowledgments

The author would like to thank the following publications where some of these poems first appeared, though occasionally in a different form:

The American Journal of Poetry: "Avenging Eve" and
        "Laundry Duty, 3 p.m."
Barren Magazine: "Slingshot Prophecies"
Birmingham Arts Journal: "Vacation Crush, 1992"
Cigar City Poetry Journal: "To a Cautious Son, 13" and
        "To the 41 Undiscovered"
Cutleaf: "Disowning the Country," "Inland: A Breakup Letter,"
        and "The Poem You Need"
Deep South: "My Grandfather's Exhibit"
Driftwood Press: "Lawn Bodies"
Fantastic Floridas: "Crooked Bones" and "Typewriter Thief"
Louisiana Literature: "Creek Wading with a Young Son"
The Medical Literary Messenger: "Red the Cartographer,"
        "Sylvia," and "Preacher Earl"
The New Southern Fugitives: "Tractor Ghosts" and
        "Whittling Lessons from an Absentee Father"
One: "The Dying Angler's Timepiece"
Open: Journal of Arts and Letters: "Biohazard Summer"
Poetry South: "Dust Workers" and "Before We Moved"
Rue Scribe: "Abandonment Lessons"
Shot Glass Journal: "Violin Boy" and "My Father's Funeral Tent"
South 85 Journal: "Absence Lights"
South Florida Poetry Journal: "The Farm Poet's Lament"
Speckled Trout Review: "Climbing Cemetery Trees"
Steel Toe Review: "The Farm I've Willed You"
Sweet Tree Review: "Craft Men"
Tampa Review: "Statue Boys"

Special thanks also to the Lanier Library in Tryon, North Carolina, for awarding the 2021 Sidney Lanier Poetry Prize to "Ode to Inherited Ties."

ABOUT THE AUTHOR

JOHN DAVIS JR. is a native Floridian who grew up on a citrus farm. His poetry has appeared in dozens of literary journals internationally, with notable features in *The Common* online, *Tampa Review, The American Journal of Poetry, Saw Palm, Nashville Review,* and numerous others. He has garnered many awards for his writing over the years, including the 2021 Sidney Lanier Poetry Prize. He is also the author of four previous collections of poems. He holds an MFA and teaches English in the Tampa Bay Area.